T0147609

BLACK AND WHITE

Love is the loudest voice.

BY   VICTOR L. SCHWARTZ

iUniverse, Inc.
New York   Bloomington

Copyright © 2010 by Victor Lewis Schwartz

All rights reserved. No part of this book may be used or reproduced by any means, graphic, electronic, or mechanical, including photocopying, recording, taping or by any information storage retrieval system without the written permission of the publisher except in the case of brief quotations embodied in critical articles and reviews.

iUniverse books may be ordered through booksellers or by contacting:

iUniverse
1663 Liberty Drive
Bloomington, IN 47403
www.iuniverse.com
1-800-Authors (1-800-288-4677)

Because of the dynamic nature of the Internet, any Web addresses or links contained in this book may have changed since publication and may no longer be valid. The views expressed in this work are solely those of the author and do not necessarily reflect the views of the publisher, and the publisher hereby disclaims any responsibility for them.

ISBN: 978-1-4502-3769-7 (sc)
ISBN: 978-1-4502-3808-3 (hc)
ISBN: 978-1-4502-3805-2 (ebook)

Printed in the United States of America

iUniverse rev. date: 8/19/2010

Dedication

To all of the black and white people

Foreword

I am prolife. I am pro-Israel, and I am pro-Jesus.

I. - Black and White

It's better if we all get along.

Just go with the seasons.

I gave myself all the bad labels, but now I am new. I am a blank slate; you can be, too.

President Barack Obama.

Life is like a rose—the thorns, the stem, the flower.

Today, we have to make life like the stem.

Like the stem means things are okay.

This is a gift; life is a gift.

I know a guy who is always happy, and I just figured out how he does it. He accepts life like the rose, the thorns hurt, and the stem are normal ... and the flower is ecstatic. He accepts it ... and God. If we accept life as the rose, we will always be happy. Life isn't always supposed to be one way ... and we've got some flowers coming.

So we'll be okay.

Okay?

There will be peace in all of our hearts when we are the same economically.

The only way we will be the same economically is when we love each other.

We don't love each other because we are too busy with guilt, anger, loneliness, and confusion.

I married a brown woman, and I am white.

So, you see, I'm in it for myself. Maybe I can help you along the way.

I want it to work.

God does, too.

So let's love each other; we don't have to be perfect. Okay, I'm in.

I hope this book can be like Disney. Disney is like perfect.

I think people are like perfect.

They are humble.

You never know how life is going to be. Let's be together.

I don't know what I can do for us. And I'll do what I can. Blame and shame are getting old. We can do anything we want to. What do we want to do? Do we know we have a choice? We do. It's called now.

Let's attack our problems, not each other.

I love people.

—Victor

I—Black and White

Let's have a moment of silence for the past.

I can't wait any longer. I love you.

Let us have full joy in the present.

The good thing about marriage is you get to be yourself, so let's be ourselves with each other.

Love is natural; it will come. The slow wheels of togetherness are still turning. Still turning.

The future is limitless.

The future is ours.

Do we want to overcome?

Or are we done?

I'm ready.

Take your time.

I'll be waiting for you.

I'll be waiting for you with a smile.

Let's go hiking.

Let's go hiking with my friend, Herb. Herb is the trail master.

We have never seen the future, but I have.

It is nice. We'll be together like mice … going for the water, of which there is an endless supply—so drink up little munchkin, let your heart touch the sky.

We are here. There is no one over there, so let's enjoy our hair. There's no need to be scared anymore.

It was fear.

It is solved.

Go to 7-11.

Go to McDonalds.

Wherever you go, there you are.

You are good.

What do you want to do?

Me, too.

Let's do it together forever.

History need not be in the present.

The present need be in the present.

There is more to gain than our own race.

Fear of what?

Slavery?

Our president is brown.

We're here! "We did it."

We can make it.

I've seen it.

I see it.

Don't think you're the only one.

We all feel this way.

Don't we?

Go for it!

I am.

Get over yourself.

I got over myself.

Now let's go the rest of the way.

Let's make music together.

We may think it's too hard. Love is easy. We've been trying too hard. Let it happen. We'll all sleep better ... forever.

If we could survive our past, how easy would it be to love each other? It can't be worse than what we've got! It is getting better. This book is to you what jumper cables are to a car.

The solution is nothing.

We've arrived.

It's over—whatever "it" means to you.

It's a beginning—

Barack Obama as president,

Me, as his citizen.

I'm not afraid of you anymore.

So are you afraid of me?

Zero.

I make my mistakes, but this book is not one of them.

I think it can really help people.

Grace.

Any problem can be overcome.

I have bipolar disorder

I haven't looked at the fact that grace keeps me alive—God's grace.

God's grace is going to bring white people and black people together.

Greed and envy have divided us.

Love and duct tape are going to keep us together.

Anything is possible.

What do you want? Get it. Anything is possible when you believe it—so believe it.

Believe me.

We can appreciate ourselves.

The only thing that teaches me anything is love.

So let me love you.

Oh, by the way, 60 percent of the people who voted for Barack Obama were white, so my work is easy.

How to zero a fear?

This is what I do:

Let fear go to zero.

Anything is possible.

We can forgive each other for any sin.

Jesus can forgive us for any sin.

The black people are good, and the white people are good.

Good.

Problem → (transition) → solution.

Don't love myself → (learning to love myself) → love myself.

I love white people.

If you are black, you have to love black people.

I like myself the way I am.

I love myself before I love another.

The word for loving myself: Me.

The word for loving everyone: We.

I'm really good the way I am.

I do whatever I want to do.

This is being myself.

My way is my best way.

Your way is your best way.

Individuality is good.

You can't have togetherness unless you have individuality.

So before I love my race, I love myself.

This is the solution to race love.

I care about myself.

I care for myself.

Do you?

Maybe we'll make it.

Maybe opens doors.

Our hearts can speak to each then through prayer.

It's just a little something.

Life is not easy, but it can be.

Love yourself … before anyone.

No more guilt. Amen.

If we can accept our imperfections, we can accept ourselves, and we can accept each other.

I accept my imperfections.

Life is going on.

Life has gone on.

Life will go on.

It is a gift.

We're not going to feel confident all of the time, so we might as well feel confident in general.

We all have purpose.

Let us be that purpose.

We can hang out together, grab a coffee together, vent, piss each other off, and love each other. It won't be perfect, so we might as well try now. It will be better. It will feel better ... so goes the world.

Let's say hi to each other.

I am a sociology major. Now I know why. I love people, can't get enough of them. I am even one of them. I am one of us. *I am one of us.*

We all are important, and we are each important; contribute.

Change with life, or life will change without you.

We have skills.

Change doesn't hurt us; not changing does, only because we have a lot to look forward to. Not just big change, little change is good, too. *Change is good.*

What we reject is how flawed we are, but that part of us is beautiful. That's what makes us a society. If we accept how flawed we are, we can find love—accepting each other and ourselves as we are.

It is hard, but possible. So let's do it. I'm afraid, too. That's not stopping me. I married a black woman. Now I want to marry you (everyone).

None of what we went through makes us bad people. We are good people trying to socialize. We will do fine. We are different. So what? Why should we suffer?

We're all in the same love boat anyway … Christian, Jewish, Muslim, etc.

Put everyone up, no matter what. It's not okay to love a few people and call yourself a lover of people. You have to love everyone if you want to call yourself a lover of people. Then you can truly love yourself.

A lack of love is no one's fault. The only solution is to love—mixed family love. Love can win if I make it, choose it, and love it.

People can't help what they go through. I don't know why. Maybe we can't handle it. Don't worry.

It's okay if we don't know why we're stressed. It's okay. Who cares?

The only reason we put each other down is because of how small we feel, so put yourself up all of the time. Watch how well you feel. You will love others because you love yourself. That's why.

People aren't perfect. I accept everyone. Sure, people are going to piss me off, and after I calm down, I accept everyone again. It is the same thing with accepting ourselves. We feel guilty, deny ourselves of love, and we come to love ourselves again. I care again.

Don't let anyone put you down—not even yourself.

I want to be a servant. I want to be the Lord's servant. I've got the heart.

We have to move.

We need to move.

I take care of myself equally well as I take care of others.

Things die in this life; things live in heaven.

The two passions I have on earth are to love myself and to love everyone.

The only one who delivered me this task is Jesus.

Thank you, Lord.

We shouldn't learn from history. We should make history.

Do what you want.

It's not too late.

Be yourself.

I am.

Everything comes down to us, testing our love for each other.

"Is it true you love me?"

We do this by first fearing each other and then by yelling at each other. When no one yells back, we feel loved.

The funny thing is that we do love each other, and we don't believe it. Take your time and believe it. It's true. Oh, and by the way, we love ourselves.

Enjoy.

I love you as much as I love myself. Just in case you're wondering, that's totally true.

It's okay to love yourself and others. Love yourself first. And give your life to your friends.

It would be bad to win the fight and lose the friendship. So don't fight. Try something else.

Love heals the boat.

Family is good.

For the first time in my life, I like challenges.

I'm not afraid.

I do it myself. When there's a problem, I do it myself. The solution?

That's okay; we'll work it as it is.

Life is one time. Don't worry about it.

People get upset; we get over it.

Don't try and deny your feelings. Accept your feelings.

People solve their own problems. No one knows this. All they need is support. White people support black people. Black people give white people support.

Problems are just solutions in disguise. After you have the solution, there is no more problem. Our minds are free to think about hope.

When you give your love away, you get back more.

The more love you have, the less love people can take away.

Just love everyone in.

Every decision of mine is mine; I choose Jesus Christ just for me.

If you're not used to making decisions, it feels awkward. But you can get good at it. Choose yourself. Choose the opposite race. Choose your own race. You'll be happier.

I will.

It is the choice to do what you want, not what you fear.

What we do by habit is strong.

But we are stronger. We must not learn from history. We must make history.

I am.

You are.

Are we happy with our choices?

If not, think about it and choose what you want—what YOU want.

I know change is up for me. I'm up for change.

I can decay or choose life.

I choose life.

I choose for everyone to have life, black and white, together … forever. Alive! Heart to heart.

Life is tough.

We have to be disappointed at times. This hurts.

And it is good sometimes.

And it is normal other times.

I'll take normal most of the time.

Forget history; we don't need it.

Let's make the present how we want it to be.

It's just love. More or less normal.

I'll take normal.

I have bipolar disorder.

I need some stability.

I believe in peace.

It's not that I don't believe in war; I believe in peace.

It's okay, I accept me.

Do this for yourself.

You'll believe in peace because you'll be at peace with yourself.

Our insecurities got us this far; our securities will get us the rest of the way. Love is the security; we can trust it.

You're good the way you are; I'm good the way I am. It's a relief because we don't have to do anything … except to choose love. This is new. This is brand new.

If we are all uncomfortable, we will all be comfortable.

Make it so everyone makes it.

Trust is important.

We can have trust. Trust someone you almost don't. This is how trust is created then built on. Trust yourself, then build on it; make it stronger. Do the same for other people.

Be found out by yourself and by other people.

We are going to trust ourselves. We are going to trust each other.

We are black and white; we are out of sight.

Basically, we all feel small.

We all want to be accepted by people.

But we don't want to accept each other because we are scared. They will love us, and we will love them.

Go to it.

Talk.

Do.

Learn.

Burn the past.

The past is our bondage.

The present is our future.

Enjoy your life.

Our lives.

We can do what we want. We can. If we do, we'll be happy. We will.

We are all people.

Help yourself first.

Help someone else second.

This is the way.

But if you are okay, put yourself last.

This is good: I am alive!

Because I feel alive, I always feel young. I will always feel this way.

Four is the number, the human number.

Love is the way.

I know better.

My life showed me this.

My better judgment told me this.

I love myself.

I love you.

What I've learned is that I've make mistakes. Good inventions come from making mistakes.

We fear being judged.

We judge as a solution.

It's in our imagination.

It's false.

God loves us. I love us.

Bipolar disorder sucks.

I want to be okay with everyone.

I want to make everyone okay with me.

I'm okay with me.

I'm okay with you, whoever you are.

On my tombstone, you can write, "I love myself."

Sometimes you don't have to do anything.

There are ways.

There are solutions.

There are problems.

Life is good.

Then I'll be the better servant.

I can love people.

People can love me.

Learn how to be a servant and learn how to be served—world peace.

Life can be better than we think it can be.

We all have different fears. Find out what they are. Get over them.

Some of our fears are white people; some of our fears are black people.

When slavery was a reality, we had a right to be afraid—black people of slavery … white people of God's judgment. At this point, all of our fears are in our heads. So choose.

If you make the wrong choice, choose again.

We already know how to say hi to people of our own race.

Hi, how are you doing?

We can say it to people of a different race.

I go over all of the problems.

Yes, you can too.

Social Networking.

Socializing.

Forget the problem.

Go with the solution.

And then embrace new problems.

You and I are the solution.

I do what I think is right.

So let's ask for each other's help.

We can help each other?

Yes.

Yes.

Obama.

We've got it. I've got it. You've got it.

I've seen it in my family.

Society is just like my family.

I've seen it.

It will all work out.

Society is my family … my extended family.

A choice is trust.

When I accepted myself, I took the bad with the good.

My friend, Tulio, does this, and so does my friend, Alex.

I accept my family by taking the bad with the good.

I accept my friends by taking the bad with the good.

I accepted everyone by taking the bad with the good.

Everyone is accepted by me, Victor Lewis Schwartz.

Do it your way.

Assertiveness.

I do it my way. This is just my way.

I'm good with society.

Society is good with me.

I want society to be good with society.

I want society to be good with societies.

It's not easy to be racially liberated, but if we are, then there is nothing to worry about.

I am racially liberated.

It's safe. Go for it.

Once everyone is racially liberated, there is nothing to worry about.

Obama is president. This is an example of racial liberation.

When you think about it, it is hard for two people to get along. Imagine a whole society? Societies? A globe? We can do it. I know we can we can. We'll feel awkward, but we can. Later, it won't be awkward. Then it'll be peaceful. Good luck.

One last thing—we can agree and disagree. This is love; this is family, and we're all family. I want to experience it. I will. We will. Let it happen for you, if you want it. You've got me.

I love you whether you agree with me or disagree with me or don't know what to do.

We all disagree and agree. We all agree on water and food. It's okay to disagree on other things. This is not a barrier to love.

I disagree with my wife on some things, but we agree on love.

We spend time on ourselves, and we spend time on each other.

We have to spend time gradually on other races.

I've got a beautiful family with two races.

I've seen the light; there's nothing to fear.

Races are good. We're in the clear.

We will all be friends.

It will be called trust.

I want to make a friendship movement.

It will be outside of religion.

It will be outside of race.

It will be outside of gender.

It will have a good place.

We're all insane.

We stay apart because of the color of skin?

Why?

I don't know.

Do you?

If we want to get together, then we can stay together. We can do this. I know we can.

Jewish, Christian, Muslim, all of us can love one another.

Anything for love.

AND

It's so hard for this book to work because we cling to our religions, and we cling to our races. I say cling to your religion and cling to your race and cling to other people's religions and cling to other people's races. It's all and, and, and.

People are trying hard to love one another.

And what do we do?

We polarize and unitize and utilize our abilities to help the poor.

But don't blame the rich, because they might get an itch to help you.

Accept yourself as you are. Accept each person as he or she is.

We categorize people. The solution is to disperse people. Don't see the groups; see the person. We are afraid of the groups, not the people who make them up. So think about it.

My faults are okay. People's faults are okay. We can still have a good time. Let's have a good time. How are you?

Me? I'm good.

Accepting people is good.

Having people accept us is good.

Think about the possibilities.

I officially go for it.

You just be completely yourself.

I'll just be completely myself.

Together we'll be ourselves.

Together we'll be free and bonded simultaneously—black people helping white people, white people helping black people.

We don't have to end up where we started out.

Do you see what I mean?

Your will and your heart are everything when you're ready, not before that.

Life's too short for acting. Start your engines. Put it in first, and proceed toward love.

I'll just take it light, no guilt. God's got a place for me. I'll find it.

I'm comfortable with love and Jesus.

We all make it work. God is the author. We are the viewers.

Dear Jesus, please steer me toward good people.

—Victor

II—About Solutions

It's got to work for all of us. We have to try different solutions when things don't work.

We will make it.

That's why we need the solutions.

We don't have to be smart to think of them.

I know I'm not. I just know what I know.

And then, there's what I figure out. You are the same way.

You have to allow yourself to think of solutions.

Together, we will think of all of the solutions to our problems.

We have to charge each other for our solutions.

We call this process working.

However, because we invent our solutions we have a better time doing it.

This is going to be good.

The Internet will speed up our ability to help people and our ability to help ourselves by being paid.

We can be heroic.

That is the mission—to be heroic.

This makes us feel better about ourselves.

Work is not about submitting or dominating.

It is about getting the job done.

And we all can do that, however, in different ways.

We need the different ways because we have so many different people with different problems.

So we need different solutions.

We can only think when we think we're not smart.

Sometimes the stupid answer is the answer to the whole thing.

Don't doubt yourself.

We make mistakes, but we learn from them.

We need to remember everything over time.

Nothing was that bad, except Satanists.

A lot of things were good.

Most things were good.

I'm talking about my life.

If something can't work, we'll work it out another way.

We've got one life.

Make it good.

Do this by working with solutions.

We make the solutions. There are always problems. Solving
problems is our working.
This is good.

Life is beautiful.

Business—it has to work out for both of us.

Life and business—they have to work out for all of us.

Life—it has to work out for each of us.

A law of business: It has to work out for everyone but us before it
will work out for us. So get good at solving problems.

Trust me. Trust yourself.

Each of us is smart.

Believe in yourself.

I believe in myself.

I still need to believe in myself more.

This will take time.

I've got time.

This is what I want to do.

I want to solve people's problems and make a comfortable living from it.

So far, I want you to do it, too.

I did for people what I could do.

Now it's time for people to do for me what they can do ... by buying this book. I appreciate it. Do your own thing.

You can do what you want.

You have to tell yourself you can.

That's what I had to do ... and it worked.

It will work for you, too. We can make it. We can all make it.

Yeah, we can all make it.

The question is: When?

Whenever we are ready is my answer.

We must have patience.

It took me twenty-three years to get this good.

I wrote to myself. It is important to me. It always was. It always will be. Myself, that is.

I want you to care about yourself, too ... in the highest level possible. And we all will make it.

The most important thing is that in order for me to make it, you and I must make it together. We will wait for each other. We can say no if we want to.

Yes, you can say no. Thank God.

Just when you say yes, make it count. Do something good and get paid for it.

Love is what holds it together. Love is what holds the economy together. So we do not love enough. Our economy is suffering because of that.

If I love myself more, I will make the economy better. But we don't love ourselves, so the economy sucks.

All I can control is myself.

After I got a massage, I gave a good tip. I make money in the economy. With that four-dollar tip, she can buy a slice of pizza. With the money for the slice of pizza, the pizza man can buy something. But if I stay at home and "save" money, I put a hole in the economy.

So spend money, and I will spend money on you and on your solutions ... for me ... for my problems.

It has to work out for both of us. If we want it to, it will.

I think we can all be comfortable. Our lives will be comfortable by both making money and by spending. We need both no matter what.

There needs to be an equal balance. The balance is not equal pay. The balance is how much you appreciate my solution as represented by your monetary value of payment to me.

I have to satisfy you, though, completely.

This is therapy to me—patience. Practice it.

Persevere—keep trying your goals, especially the important ones.

Patience and perseverance are like your right and left hand. You need them both. They help each other.

Keep them both forever.

Wherever I am here, I am. Do you know love? You can.

You can't have peace with war.

One depends on the other for definition.

Love is different. Love accepts the good and the bad.

With war, when peace gets bad, we rely on war. When war gets bad, we rely on peace.

Love tolerates existence. Peace does not. Peace means you've got your finger on the trigger. Love puts the gun away. It turns "weapons into plowshares." It is not perfect.

It is good. Consider love … and we just might stay around for awhile.

Love saved my life—Jesus did, too.

Love tolerates peace. Love tolerates war; love revels in love.

Love comes out of war. Love comes out of peace. So we might as well accent love.

I'll stay with love. Jesus gave me this; the Holy Spirit showed me this.

You can't control someone else, so love. This is the whole answer. Love wants everyone to love.

Our solutions are really great. We need to help each other with them.

Love can change the world. Nothing else can.

Jesus showed us love. That changed the world.

We can love; we can love; we can love, and we can love.

It's not in competition. It's in surrendering—surrendering to love.

Are you up for it?

There's no plan. You just do it.

When is not important. It is always welcomed. Only you can do it … for yourself.

Love comes from hope. And hope comes from love.

They are perpetual motion.

Love can't die.

Jesus died, but love didn't die.

I am a Christian because I love Christ.

He died for my sins to be forgiven. And they were.

So I'm writing to you about love. So Jesus doesn't have to forgive more of my sins.

I want to love you. I need your help. So does Jesus.

This is an invitation. Welcome.

I changed the world—everyday.

Love is moving. Let's move with it. This is our only choice. What do you say?

With love we can breathe. Without it we can't.

Love for ourselves and each other is what mends the economy— permanently.

So love. If someone won't love you, love someone else.

I'm just trying my best. Every day is a challenge.

Love is the smart one, and the smart one loves.

We're not perfect. So love is the cushion.

Love is the cushion I'm pushing. Do you know anyone who wants it? Maybe you?

Good luck, grasshopper!

Just love. Broken hearts heal; mine did three times.

New love is born into pure love that will last forever—my wife.

Love is better than force. We have more options. Find them; sell them. I will buy them.

"Be the best you can be."—My wife.

We have the whole rest of our lives to live. Lose weight. Quit smoking.

Whatever you want, you can do it. Believe it. Live it. Achieve it. Do it.

Do you know Jesus' love? Jesus is everything. Salvation is only through him.

The truth—what do you think? All of us—who do you think?

If we think we can, we can.

Get an idea, a metamorphosis from the past. Leave your old self behind; go with your new idea, in your new skin, in your new idea of yourself.

So think we can, and we all can.

Never go backward; only go forward. We're all afraid of each other. Why? Because we part?

We have no reason to be afraid of each other.

We have no reason to be afraid of ourselves.

Jesus forgives our sins.

Go to him. He is waiting with open arms. He always will be.

That's because all of us are not perfect.

So take heart; all of us have a good guide. His name is Jesus Christ.

So don't expect too much from people because they'll let you down. Expect everything from Jesus.

I'm a man of faith. I have faith in you.

Love is no one's fault.

Understanding is the way of the world. Even when I don't understand, I don't have to get it right; I just have to try.

If I do get it right, good. If I don't get it right, at least I tried. This is Jesus' love in action—understanding.

I am not afraid anymore.

If I will understand people, people will understand me.

I was going to blame kids for not being loving enough, but adults are the same way.

"Let love go, and it will come back to you." —Mike Weiss.

You can't forgive if you don't understand.

So try to understand.

I'll try to understand.

And I'll fail.

And people will appreciate my trying.

That is called love.

I love you, and I'll try.

I'll try to understand you.

I already understand me.

Try to understand. Try to understand. Try to understand yourself.

This is why Jesus Christ is the one because he is teaching us this.

We all need more understanding ... me, too.

We're all equal to Jesus.

I just had a carwash. You should get one.

III—From the Fear of Abandonment to Security in Jesus Christ

Security is great. There is no fear. Security is the focus. Security is the solution. The fear of abandonment is the problem.

My mistake was trusting my fear of abandonment. Why? Fear.

The only way to security is focusing on security. How do I know? Because, it worked for me. It always will.

It is my dream to lead the world to security. The fear of abandonment needs be replaced with security. We can all do this.

Basically, I took my own fear and solved it. Take your fear and solve it.

People with the fear of abandonment have it so long because they try to solve it by focusing on it.

The only way to stop it is to focus on security. If we focus on the fear of abandonment, we perpetuate it. We don't need to do that. Someone in this world will love you.

The fear of abandonment is caused by people leaving us. Usually more than one person leaves us.

I'm going to heal you by focusing on security. Jesus Christ showed me that security is the way. He is the security that gave me security over the fear of abandonment.

I have had a great relationship with Jesus Christ, and he now wants me to have a great relationship with myself. He gave me security in him.

Security in Jesus Christ gave me security in myself; because I trust Jesus Christ, he lets me see that I am wise to trust him. So I trust Jesus forever.

This is the only way; this is the only way to heaven.

Jesus Christ is my security. So I follow Jesus Christ to have security. He shows me all this. He shows me all this through the Bible.

You can do this as I did; just ask Jesus to help you. Yes, you guessed it … He will. It doesn't matter how long you've suffered; I've suffered twenty-three years.

Now I have security. I am secure.

Thank you, Jesus Christ. Amen. Hallelujah!

We're going to get that house on the water in Kings Point, New York.

It's hard to be positive, but Jesus Christ is the only way to optimism. That's how I went from the fear of abandonment to security.

Security … Jesus Christ.

No matter how bad you are, Jesus Christ can forgive you. Isn't this great?

The fear of abandonment is cruel. It is the devil hurting us. That's the only reason.

Jesus is stronger than the devil. Jesus can break the chain of fear.

Jesus tells us not to trust fear but to trust security. Do you see the difference?

You can do it. Jesus wants to help, so do I want to help? Security.

I used to be an atheist with my fear of abandonment.

I accept Christ, and I have security. I always have security. I always will because I accept Christ.

So, think about two things: Christ and security.

You have to like Christ before you can like yourself. When you like Christ, he lets you like yourself, respectively.

I don't have the fear of abandonment anymore

I have security and the longing for Christ and the longing for you to long for Christ like I do.

I know this is the right way; I used to be an atheist.

There's hope for you, definitely. "God can do all things."

Fear can really paralyze you.

I suffered from the fear of abandonment.

I suffered from the fear of homosexuality; I was molested as a kid. And my mother put me up for adoption. That's how I had the fear of homosexuality and the fear of abandonment.

Now I'm eating a yogurt.

I never thought I'd get over my fear.

I did. You can, too.

Let Jesus Christ guide you. I never thought I was good enough to get over the fear abandonment. But Jesus did think I was good enough.

Now I do. I think.

I'm good enough to have security.

I used to be so down on myself. I tried to solve my fears by focusing on them.

Now I focus on Christ and on security in Christ. He is the only way to heaven.

Check the Bible's New Testament. I did, and I believe it.

And I am saved. I am going to heaven. I will make mistakes, but I am not mistaken about this.

I want you to go to heaven, too.

Jesus, thank you for the possibility of life, amen.

I was first in a bicycle store. I noticed that it was too hard for me to do that for a living. That's why I write for a living.

It's going to be good to get older. I'm watching old people, and they look like they're enjoying themselves.

Christ is wonderful, though. I'm not afraid of getting older. I'm a writer who likes bicycle riding.

I don't want to be fat. I don't want to be fat, so I'll bike ride. I'll relearn bicycle riding. Jesus will show me how. Right now, I'm fat.

I love fat people, too.

My wife, I just love her.

People who had the fear of abandonment have to relearn life, so it doesn't matter if you're fat. Do what you can do at your own pace.

Say what you want to say, but let the words come out of your lips. You're tired? Stop. You're bored? Go.

Say what you want to say ... not what you should say or what you think people want you to say.

I just thought about it. Being fat is not my problem; not exercising is my problem. I'm fat because I don't exercise.

I'm so proud of plumbing; I think that is one of the greatest inventions.

Someone's got to stick up for Him. It might as well be me.

We're all the same, but if Christ saved you, you are going to heaven. Christ is the only way to heaven.

The devil will tell you otherwise. The Bible will tell you that Jesus Christ is the only way to heaven.

I want you to go to heaven, so I tell you Jesus is the way and the light.

He didn't let you down, so don't let Him down. He died for you. He died for your sins to be forgiven.

I have Christ. I am fulfilled. I just want to praise Christ! I'm for Jesus Christ. He's the best.

I like the Christ in me.

I want Christ to save you. Just pray that you need a savior. You recognize that you are separated from God by sin and that you want Jesus to come into your heart and cleanse you from all of your sins.

Ask for guidance to lead you to someone who can help you with that.

That's it! Are you excited? I am for you ... for us.

God's got plans for you if you want to make them happen.

My job is to please Jesus because he gave me a wife. But I should please Jesus way above that. I should try and please my wife.

I love my dog.

Jesus saved me from a suicide attempt. He can do great things. He cured me from mental illness. He did it through Lucinda Bassett's CDs. Thank you, Jesus.

The best part about being saved is just hanging in there. All good things come from there (here, in my case).

And when Jesus Christ is on your side, you will win at everything.

IV—What Is Jesus For?

Helping a homeless person is on Jesus's menu. Trying not to sin is on Jesus's menu. I'm fat, so I'm thinking of a menu, but Jesus will take care of that.

Jesus asks that we give 10 percent of what we make, so the bigger the 10 percent we give is, the bigger the 90 percent is. We should give because we want to, not for gain. When we do that, Jesus rewards us.

A car is a false sense of security. Jesus Christ is a true sense of security. He can take you to heaven forever.

The only way is love; and love in Christ is the only true love.

I love people deeply in a way that Christ only understands.

People who need patience need Christ.

I'm back in the cycle for bicycle riding. I'm the limit.

This is the end of the fear of abandonment for me.

I've been expecting too much from myself and from everyone.

Content.

William Shakespeare.

Calm is life.

The reason why we can't get along is because we both think we can't do enough for each other to make up for slavery. It was traumatic. We are still messed up. We need to deserve each other.

What do we do now? That's the question. Realize we deserve each other—that's the answer. Trauma is meant to be gotten over.

Black and white, that is right.

This is right.

Do what you want to do with this knowledge.

We deserve each other; I give it the okay. I give the okay for us to be friends.

You have to give the okay, too.

Take my time at work.

Control.

One thing you can control is C. C represents life. A represents a want, and B represents attaining the thing you want.

We're no good at waiting. We have to get good at waiting. By extending C in time, we will have patience.

I believe our economy is in bad shape because we always got what we want. We also got it when we wanted it. No good.

What if we don't get what we want when we want it? We will experience turbulent Cs (lives). We will feel like we will never get there if we wait.

We have to live in C. Things come and go, but our life remains constant.

Jesus Christ showed me this solution. I show it to you.

If we learn again how to wait for something, we will be all right. Extend your C.

A (want) $\rightarrow$ C (wait) $\rightarrow$ B (Get what you want)

Right now, patience is a small thing, but it is the **solution**.

The good news is that we have a good life (C). The other good news is I'm going to show you how to live it.

Add time to your C. Add time to your goals. You're more likely to attain your goals if you give yourself more time to achieve them.

You're not failing to attain your goals. You are not giving yourself time to attain them. So relax. You're on time. You'll get there when you get there.

So what can we do while we wait? Something else. Write a book—that's what I do. But you do what you want to do. Breathe.

We weren't breathing because we got so used to getting what we want without breathing.

I don't want to blame anyone. I just want to fix it. And we will fix it.

Patience is the missing ingredient in our lives, and because it is in our lives, it is in our lives; it is in our economy. We lack patience in our economy.

We'll make it. We just have to have patience. This is my fault, too. I need more patience, so we'll grow at it together. This is going to be fun. The best part is we'll get what we want.

Our waiting for what we want will lead us to do one thing—appreciate it.

If we just get what we want, we will take it for granted.

So the economy will fix itself. A and B will become farther apart for all of us. Want and get will be farther apart. Appreciation will go up.

People will be happier. So, yep, you guessed it—getting something deserved brings us joy.

The only way to get appreciation is to want something and to wait for it. We'll get our chance.

So we didn't fail! No, we just messed up. We are alive; that's the main thing. Dust yourself off and take the next chance.

The economy can be fixed by overusing on our lives. Don't spend extra. Don't spend less. Spend what you need and call it a day.

We've got our priorities wrong. It's not our passions like our blackberry that we must cling to. It's our Jesus Christ that we must cling to. Oh yes.

I cling to him, and my family is fine. That's why. I could tell you stories, but instead, you cling to Christ and watch your life float.

Get into life. You can get into life only with Jesus. There will be a new economy with Jesus Christ. He's in charge of money. I'm on his side. I'm secure. He's yours.

Jesus Christ is not here to punish you. He is here to save your soul. Only he can do this.

Oh, and about the economy—if it got good, it can get better. Spend on what you need, and the economy will pick up speed.

We never gave ourselves time to breathe.

Set your life on indefinite and watch your life begin. Don't expect the good; expect to live for once.

Life is the thing in between things. Let's form on life itself. Everything else will come later. It is not attaining; it is maintaining.

So basically we will be forced to increase our life and appreciate things more.

We can avoid hitting rock bottom by spending on what we need. This will keep you going.

What is better than being rich or poor? Keep going, maintaining. You will get what you give.

There will always be a solution with Jesus Christ.

It sounds so crazy that something as easy as waiting could be the answer, but I tell you, if you want, you will get.

We aren't getting because we aren't waiting, so wait and get, please. This goes for drawing, blank lines, editing, etc.

Let the rest of our lives be waiting.

And we will live a little while we're waiting, and ultimately we're waiting for heaven if we're saved by Jesus Christ.

The whole lie that the devil put before us is that the more we get, the happier we will be.

We have it all, and we want more. More isn't making us happier, so let's just maintain.

Also, with cars, faster is not better. The speed limit is better.

The solution to weight is to maintain. We need to eat the amount to maintain. That's all.

The whole of life is between wanting and attaining. I call it living.

I love us, and I'm going to help us in Jesus' name.

So the devil lied to us. If more is better, why are we in a recession? More is worse; comfortable is enough.

We don't appreciate what we have, why would we want more?

Get that out of our heads. Just right is enough. Be happy with what we have.

We all need to stay afloat with no water in the boat. We have enough money in the economy to do this.

We can give 10 percent to the poor, or whatever we need to give, staying afloat with no water in the boat. It could have been you who needed help, so help people happily in Christ's name.

I'm just fooling myself by getting material things. Christ makes me happy forever... by helping people (by my helping people)

I like this more than money. This is righteous. Give it a try. With Christ it doesn't have to be easy.

What Christ showed me in life is that it should be harder because I believe in Jesus Christ. The safest lane for you is going to be the slow lane.

How to deal with impatience is to get there later or not at all.

We need each other. Love is right for all of us, for all of us we need each other. Love is right. Patience takes time.

The future is better than the past. The present is better than the past was. White people, as you love black people as you love white people, love yourself.

It is our responsibility, not our fault. No one's perfect. Having a black and white president is only a beginning to our love for each other. Do you see? Do you see it happening? It sees you happening.

Just because of our love for Jesus Christ, we should appreciate each other more.

The biggest challenge is for us to accept and love each other, as Jesus said, or what would be the reward? If it were easy, there would be no reward.

Time goes on without a problem. Why should we have a problem? No time is wasted.

It's not that I'm better than anymore. I just have Jesus Christ.

V—On Giving, Love, and Respect

When you want something, you have to give.

Weakness and strength are good.

I accept not perfect.

Just keep living.

I'm strong enough to submit.

The best part of life is leaning to submit to oneself.

Being respected is a very important part of life.

I like Lonnie.

The best way for a therapist and patient to be is to want to learn everything from each other.

Nobody so perfect, but together we will learn what we need to know.

In order to be respected, we have to be loved.

Fear is not respect.

I can't pass all of the tests. I'm not qualified.

Love is respect.

Love can lead to respect, if the love is true.

After my book comes out, I'll charge sixty-five dollars per hour for my friendships.

The only way to win a fight is not to have one.

I love everyone, but few deserve me. Marriage is just a conversation; so start talking.

Staying in it for love.

The good of marriage is to act over both the fear of ourselves and the fear of our partners.

Love her to death.

The whole talk solution to the world.

No one knows everything, so you might as well get to know a lot of people.

Marriage really doesn't have to be perfect. You can have problems, and it can all work out.

When you trust someone fully, it is a great thing.

Anger is fear.

If you know how messed up I am, you know how normal you are.

I'm going try my best and don't worry about the rest.

Just because I want to.

I'm making progress with Lonnie.

Jesus is my friend.

Things don't go always as planned, but they go.

It's not me or you; it's both of us, tailgating.

You're got to work for love.

Everything worked out.

Love is stronger than judgment.

The best thing I did in life was give up my fears. Of course, Jesus is more important than this.

People who believe in Satan are like a bird without wings, only worse.

Anger is fear. Fear can be overcome with love.

A lot of the things you think are good are bad.

People who talk to themselves—those people are the normal people. Everyone else is pretending they don't.

We're not perfect, but we act like we are. That's why we talk to ourselves. We need Jesus. That's the only way.

Work is generally to keep people happy.

Jesus is the only way—this leads to heaven.

I don't have any problems. I have Jesus.

Christ and truth get me and my wife over every hurdle.

I trust myself, my wife, Herb Erwin, my adoptive parents, my birth mother, and Mike Drake fully. Chris and Dad Stonelake are getting closer to us.

Money is easy. Jesus Christ is hard.

For me, with bipolar disorder, I wait for the good times because the bad times are so bad.

This illness is trying to kill me, and I stay alive for myself, for my wife, for my kids, and for Jesus.

The fear of abandonment is nothing to worry about.

The past is no indication of the future.

The present is what it is.

The present is not to be feared.

The present is to be understood.

Fear is a choice that we don't have to make.

I choose not to fear.

All of the addictions are fears.

Choose not to fear, and you'll beat the addiction.

The addiction is an attempt to stop a fear. It doesn't work, and that's why it's called an addiction. Choose not to fear. You'll get there.

Fear is a feeling that sometimes isn't true.

Just enjoy being alive.

A lack of love hurt me, and a presence of love healed me.

I am very happy because of the love I have in my life. I have to love myself.

I want the best for myself.

I want the best for you.

Loving myself is really a good thing. As I love myself, I love others.

When I'm ready, I'll get into shape.

It's a challenge to love myself. I think my bipolar disorder has a lot to do with this.

With everyone, it's all about love. We're all chasing love.

Baseball is always good.

Special thanks to the bartender at the Little Neck Inn.

Even though we all make mistakes, we can all love each other.

Special thanks to Eddie Bieleckly.

Jesus loves me.

We have love together … starting with me. I love us.

Respect yourself. Respect others.

By helping other races, I will be content.

The people with the biggest problems have the biggest success rates, but only with Christ.

Don't take it personally.

If your goal is not control, if your goal is self-mastery, don't worry about being controlled. Control yourself.

If you want to control yourself, simply stop trying to control everyone else.

I shouldn't want to control other people.

Control yourself, not me.

Patience and tolerance and love.

More love.

Maude is good, so I am a victor.

No one has control, except of themselves.

I take no joy in hurting myself.

I take no joy in hurting anyone.

 I do what I want to do.

Don't be afraid to submit.

When it comes to men with their wives, the safest position for men is to not take a position.

When a man is offensive to his wife, she attacks him.

The safest position, that is, the best way to keep your wife happy is not to scare her. She won't scare you either.

And the man leads ... whether he wants to or not.

A person's station in life is not important. What he does with that station is important.

Christ doesn't care about what you're going to do.

Everything in its time; but if you don't have Jesus Christ, nothing in its time.

Last is surely the best.

Black people were angry about slavery. They were right. We were wrong, sorry.

The Bible says the police are the guardians of our souls.

Both people and the police have to trust each other.

We have to pay for our mistakes. We might as well learn from them. Use Jesus as your guide. That's what I do.

The reason why rich people don't give money to the poor is because the devil deceives them by telling them that Jesus wants them to give all of their money to the poor and then they will be poor themselves. Jesus asks for 10 percent, so give it with a smile.

I'm proud of myself for following Jesus.

The past is sad; the future's good.

I want to save all of the people in the world.

Everything in its time.

VI—Being Rich with Jesus

If we all lose, we all win.

Submit. All submit. All submit simultaneously. All will be the best forever.

I did this. It works. No one expects this—no one, except me.

We can't have each other without Christ.

I'm the strongest man on earth, and I'm weak. I'm strong because Christ is my strength. I'm weak because I'm a man. I'm not perfect.

We think love is a weakness. People, wake up. Christ is the only love. Christ is the only love; everything else is the devil.

Everyone should be spoiled with love.

If we don't have money, we can spoil each other with love. If we have love and money, then we really love each other.

Think about it. Be generous. Be Christ like. Accept help. It comes from Christ. People just help.

Everyone should be spoiled with money—no favoritism. Christ is making this happen. Thank him; don't thank me. I just love him. He loves me, too, and he loves you, too. A woman gave away her last bit of money. We can give, too.

Rich people are rich. Just imagine if everyone were rich. When your problems are solved, you are rich. Help people solve their problems, so they can be rich. It's no problem.

Let it be a pleasure to pay people for their services.

Let it be a pleasure to accept money for giving your services.

If you're alive, you're rich, so appreciate everything from there.

Jesus asks only for the possible; only we make things impossible.

When it comes to getting what I want, it's okay if I don't get it. I have enough of what I need.

We all have different systems. We're all right. But Jesus tempers us. He helps us get along with each other. We can get along, all of us on earth, but we need Jesus to temper us.

We need Jesus to help us get along, so we have a good time. You deserve the best; that's why I give you Jesus.

Just do the best you can do.

My life works out.

Your life works out.

Our lives work out.

Isn't this great?

My life is getting better.

There was no way I could work before.

Now I can't work.

Later, I don't know if I can work.

I can write.

Jesus Christ is great.

I hate cursing.

Jesus gave me a seed that will grow into two trillion dollars.

I love life.

I will keep one billion dollars of the two trillion. The rest will go to Haiti. My books will help people. My books will help my family.

I love Dr. Nass.

I love Lonnie Tinter.

I love myself

I love my family.

It's okay to be a little hungry.

I believe Jesus Christ made my dreams come true.

Wherever I am, there I'll be.

I am better.

I can't go backwards; I have to go forwards.

I can live.

I want to live.

I am getting old and loved.

I don't have to worry, no I don't at all.

I want to serve Jesus more than anything in the world.

We all think riches do not have to do anything; therefore, we are fat. This is so far from the truth.

We should be bigger than ourselves when it comes to putting different races up to our level; it will only help us and bring more business.

My dad is suffering with gout. I am doing my best to take care of him. My mom won't get help. This is the end of his life. I am handling it pretty well. I want to get into shape. I will.

People, places, all of them are neutral zones, except Satanists.

Christ takes over all of my problems.

Without Christ, people can't handle their problems.

I will always stay with Christ.

I will always stay with my man, Christ.

With Christ, I'm amazing.

I've got no problems. I've got Christ.

My balance in life is to have my feelings and to accept them.

A man can accept his feelings … all of them, all of his feelings.

A man can cry.

One thing I don't know is why I gain weight.

One thing I know is that I love myself.

Being me isn't easy. It took me thirty-nine years to be myself. Ultimately, I was the one trying to be myself. I just accepted that—that was me. It is me. I am me. How true. I do believe we've got it made.

Summer—I look forward to you.

This is a hard one.

People are just the same. We waste our time trying to be different. Let's just be the same, love.

I'm a man.

You learn one thing at a time.

The key to the world is not to go backwards but to go forward.

I can't feel good, unless I'm right with Jesus.

I really love myself.

I don't want the fat.

I can do anything through Jesus Christ who strengthens me.

In reference to people calling me back, I've got to accept that people aren't me. Most people aren't as considerate as I am.

My life—from misery to mastery—I'm going to make it.

Sex is temporary; love is here to stay.

Long term goal: Let bicycle riding be a part of my life.

Cycle however I want to. There is no good way.

Just do it to enjoy it.

My main goal is to be a bike rider.

I'm organizing my life better than I used to.

I really want to drink less water.

No matter what, together we're in. Amen.

I was scared.

That's a fear that I don't have.

I'm starting to know me; I like what I see.

If I do what Christ needs, I'll get what I need.

No expectations lead to appreciation.

Life is okay.

It's okay to have a bad day and a good life.

I'm really happy.

When I can't handle something, I leave it up to someone else to handle it.

Different races come together in marriage and get out of the ever-troubled same race. Get out of the boxes and get into the big pool.

No expectations everything will work out.

We have a lot of problems—just kidding!

Christ helps us with this.

We have emotions. This is okay for me to deal with.

Caring is good.

Christ is the answer. He is my all in all.

I can lighten up a little.

We're a mess, no distress.

It's okay for me to care about myself fully because then I can care about everyone fully.

Being middle class is better than being a king or a queen because I can relate to other middle class people and smile for a while … forever.

It's not everything, but interracial marriage is a good thing.

As a person, I don't accept myself.

As a world, we don't accept ourselves.

So, why not?

So why?

Accept yourself before you try to accept another.

We need Christ. We need each other.

We're not getting points for rejecting ourselves, so accept everyone, including yourself.

Jesus gives me this.

I give it to you.

Life is more than money. You should enjoy yourself.

Only focus part of your time on money.

Focus on fun.

Have fun with everyone.

Oh, yeah, Jesus is good … I didn't always know.

Christ gives me attention.

I don't want attention.

I want everyone else to get attention—more than enough attention.

Accepting our own imperfections, accept ourselves and accept others.

No, we don't have to be perfect, but Jesus does. This is why I rely on him. This is the beauty of it.

I now realize I was expecting myself to be perfect.

No can do.

Nor can you.

Do you see what I mean?

I have come clean.

We're all the same in Christ's eyes.

The devil wants us to hate each other.

Hate the devil.

Love each other, black and white.

Jesus died for us on the cross.

I was once unsaved.

We're all trying to believe that we're perfect. This is our own downfall. This is our downfall. This is how the devil keeps us down. Rise with Christ and repent. We are all flawed, but Christ doesn't want us to pay. He paid for us. We need him for salvation. This is the only way to heaven, friend.

We've all got to suffer for Christ.

No problem.

I'm just happy with what I have.

Respect for Christ is most important. Only after this should we try respect of people. Lastly, we should try respect of ourselves.

Just love.

The main thing is that we have a choice ... Jesus or the devil.

Choose Jesus; I did.

The devil is eternal suffering.

Jesus is eternal joy.

I'm sure about Jesus Christ now.

He is my Lord and savior forever.

The devil will go to hell forever.

I will go to heaven forever because I'm saved.

You can be saved, too.

Read the Bible.

We need Christ; we need each other. We're all the same. It's real. Love is grand. God is great. Jesus Christ, we appreciate. All you have to do is stay with Jesus Christ

Got to wait for a pizza?

Jesus will have us appreciating it.

There's really nothing to say. It's all about Jesus Christ.

What we think of as security is not security.

Christ is security.

Money is a façade.

Christ provides in this life and in the next.

You know what people know?

People know where bathrooms are.

We should know Christ like we know where bathrooms are.

The devil is my worst enemy.

Sometimes, when I'm not paying attention, I'm just glad Jesus Christ is in charge.

Think about this: The only security is Christ. Choose it or lose it.

I've been rushing.

Don't rush.

I've slowed down for the rest of my life.

Thanks, Jesus Christ.

The whole problem is that I was rushing.

Kids and their dad.

Yes to the kids and yes to me.

The good thing about white people is that they're great. The good thing about black people is that they're great.

Slow rules.

The next time a black person is mad at you for being white, say it isn't right. Love the world.

I know I choose to go slow. We have to go slow and appreciate the newest technology. If you choose to go fast, you won't appreciate the newest technology. It will appreciate you.

Your guess is just as good as mine.

Jesus, I am trying my best.

God, I'm trying my best.

I mean well for all of us.

We've got to love.

Loving is possible with Jesus Christ.

Without him, it is not possible. Loving your family is easy. To love your enemy, you need Jesus only.

Black and white people are brothers and sisters. Better than that, we're friends.

We're really doing it.

Everyone is just as intelligent as everyone else.

But Jesus rules.

Psychology has wrecked us. Jesus will take us back.

Science has failed us.

Jesus has saved us.

The only thing that is for us is Jesus.

Even I have failed us.

We have reached the level of non-appreciation. We have everything, and we appreciate nothing. The only thing that will help us is having less. So help the poor people, and you will have less. Do it in Jesus' name.

If the end of the world comes, we have Jesus. I know the end of the world will come. I just don't know if it will be in my lifetime, so I pray and I obey Christ.

If a white person has a problem with a black person black is back.

Now I have patience and let people grow.

We need Christ. He will give us a new life. He *will* give us a new life.

Put people up.

We have to become more patient.

This is the only way.

We will do it imperfectly. Jesus will help you if you let him.

The hard part is over. Now let's party.

We have to trust ourselves. If you are white and you like a black person, go for it. Befriend him or her. Christ rules.

If you are a black person and you like a white person, go for it. Befriend him or her.

The future is literally new. We can do.

There's no one saying we can't.

I'm proud of you.

I'm proud of us.

We've come a long way.

We will go further than we've come.

Try hard.

Love people you don't love.

Love yourself.

The product of loving another race is that you love yourself.

It's similar to when a man and a woman marry.

Jesus always wins.

The good thing about my holding on to my biological parents is that I always cared.

My illness was nothing compared to my love for my parents.

To all of the people who don't believe in Jesus, I say just love, you will. I love you in advance.

I gotta love you to appraise to you that Jesus is worth it.

Truth is the way, and Jesus is the truth.

Jesus equals heaven.

No Jesus equals hell.

I love you.

Slowing down is the Christly thing to do.

Slow down and enjoy life. You know what I'm talking about. Believe in yourself; there's nothing wrong with you. Have your own ideas. That's what I did; of course, you can.

I wrote for twenty years before I believed what I was saying. Twenty years is a small price.

Patience, oh yeah.

God bless black people!

Be humble or everyone honks at you.

Be proud of righteous aspirations.

But don't be proud. Now, make mistakes. You will.

They're acceptable.

Christ will help you.

Christ is the helper.

Christ is my main helper. Second are the people who believe in Christ who help me. I help me too because I believe in Christ.

It's the hardest thing you'll ever do.

With Christ, heaven is guaranteed … if you're saved.

Tell Christ you see you are separated from God by sin and that you need Christ to make you right with God. He died on the cross for your sins to be forgiven.

Jesus died, was buried, and came to life again by rising to be at the right hand of his Father God in heaven. His kingdom will have no end. He will come again to judge the living and the dead.

If you accept Christ as your personal Lord and Savior by confessing all of this with your mouth, you are saved and will skip hell and go to heaven forever when you die or if Jesus comes first. Happy?

God Bless white people! God bless black people!

We made it.